Hi Benji!

P9-DXM-965

Saint Ignatius of Loyola

This is a true story about a man that Grandpa Pat likes to follow. Grandpa goes to a retreat every summer to learn about the things that Ignatius said to do. We hope you will enjoy the story.

We love you!
Grandma Linda
&
Grandpa Pat

Saint Ignatius of Loyola

For the Greater Glory of God

Written by
Donna Giaimo, FSP
and
Patricia Edward Jablonski, FSP

Illustrated by
Patrick Kelley

Pauline
BOOKS & MEDIA
Boston

Library of Congress Cataloging-in-Publication Data

Giaimo, Donna.
    Saint Ignatius of Loyola : for the greater glory of God / written by
Donna Giaimo and Patricia Edward Jablonski ; illustrated by Patrick Kelley.
        p.cm. — (Encounter the saints series ; 8)
        ISBN 0-8198-7043-9
    1. Ignatius, of Loyola, Saint, 1491–1556—Juvenile literature. 2. Christian
saints—Spain—Biography—Juvenile literature. [1. Ignatius, of Loyola,
Saint, 1491–1556. 2. Saints.] I. Jablonski, Patricia E. II. Kelley, Patrick,
1963– ill. III. Title. IIV. Series.
    BX4700 . L7 G53 2000
    271'.5302—dc21
                                    00-010328

"P" and PAULINE are registered trademarks of the Daughters of Saint Paul.

Copyright © 2001, Daughters of St. Paul

Published by Pauline Books & Media, 50 Saint Paul's Avenue, Boston, MA
02130–3491.

Printed in the U.S.A.

SIOL VSAUSAPEOILL9-710187 7043-9

www.pauline.org

Pauline Books & Media is the publishing house of the Daughters of Saint
Paul, an international congregation of women religious serving the Church
with the communications media.

8 9 10 11 12   25 24 23 22 21

Saint Ignatius of Loyola
For the Greater Glory of God

Saint Joan of Arc
God's Soldier

Saint John Paul II
Be Not Afraid

Saint Kateri Tekakwitha
Courageous Faith

Saint Martin de Porres
Humble Healer

Saint Maximilian Kolbe
Mary's Knight

Saint Pio of Pietrelcina
Rich in Love

Saint Teresa of Avila
Joyful in the Lord

Saint Thérèse of Lisieux
The Way of Love

Saint Thomas Aquinas
Missionary of Truth

Saint Thomas More
Courage, Conscience, and the King

*For even more titles in the
Encounter the Saints series,
visit: www.pauline.org/EncountertheSaints*

CONTENTS

1

An Unexpected Letter

"Inigo, hurry home! Your father is looking for you!"

The figure at the top of the hill waved in answer, and the servant, satisfied at having fulfilled her mission, returned to the castle.

"Your son will be here any minute, Don Beltrán," Luisa reported. "He's up on the hill."

"Now what's he doing *there*?" Señor de Loyola mumbled. "But thank you, Luisa. You may continue preparing supper."

It was late summer, 1506. The warm Castilian sun shone brilliantly on the countryside. Inigo turned once more to take in the scene. He sighed as he headed toward the castle just below. The castle he called home.

I wonder why Father wants me, he thought as he ran.

At the door he paused just long enough to brush back a strand of light hair. Beltrán de Loyola liked to see his children neat and perfectly mannered.

Inigo met an impatient Luisa in the hall, clicking her tongue that supper would be late because of him. "Your father is waiting for you, and the food is all ready. This news had better be important!" she warned.

Inigo nodded and smiled as the woman scurried toward the kitchen. "Yes, Luisa. I promise we won't be long."

Walking down the hall, Inigo again wondered what his father could want.

He stopped before an elaborately carved door and knocked.

"Come in," a voice within answered.

Inigo pushed open the heavy door. "You called for me, Father?"

"Yes. Yes. Come in."

Señor de Loyola stood by an open window holding a letter in his hand. He smiled as he motioned for his son to enter.

"I have good news for you, Inigo. Sit down."

Inigo took a seat in one of the large leather chairs. His father sat facing him.

"Take a look at this!" Señor de Loyola boomed as he leaned forward and handed Inigo the letter. "My old friend, Don Juan Velázquez, the treasurer of Castile, has asked me to send him one of my sons to act as his page. You will learn good manners and when the time comes, Don Juan will introduce you to the world of the court."

Señor de Loyola paused and studied Inigo. *God has blessed me with a wonderful family,* he thought, *a good wife—now, I'm sure, in heaven—seven sons and six daughters. But there is something special and different about this youngest son of mine. Perhaps it's his thirst for adventure, or his keen interest in chivalry and knighthood. Or maybe it's that far-off look that sometimes comes into his eyes...*

Inigo's excited voice broke into his father's thoughts.

"Father, are you choosing *me* to go to Don Juan's castle?"

"Yes, Inigo," Señor de Loyola smiled broadly. "I'm choosing you."

2

LEAVING HOME

Ever since he could remember, Inigo had wanted to be a knight...a warrior who would fight in the king's army. In his childhood he used to play court and knights with his older brothers. At that time they hadn't let him be anything but a page, or an armor-bearer at best. "But someday," he had assured them, "I'll be a knight. I promise you that!"

One of Inigo's favorite hobbies was reading novels. In their pages knights and nobles came to life. He relived their adventures over and over in his imagination. Excitement, action, even danger—these were what appealed to Inigo. His dream was to share the same kind of fame and greatness described in the novels. Now at last he was being sent to prepare for life at court!

Inigo was excited and frightened at the same time. He wanted to go, but he *would* miss his family, especially his father and Doña Magdalena.

Inigo had never really known his mother, Doña Marina. She had died when he was very young. After her death, his father had brought Inigo to the Garíns, a family that lived a short distance from the Loyola castle. Inigo had grown up there, with his father visiting him often and María de Garín caring for him as if he were one of her own children. When Inigo's older brother Martín married Magdalena de Araoz in 1498, Martín brought her to live at the family castle. Inigo went home to the castle shortly after, and Magdalena became like a second mother to him.

Magdalena wanted what was best for Inigo. But she was concerned about his leaving the family at such a young age. One night, she was unusually quiet at supper. Don Beltrán took her aside after the meal. "What is it, Magdalena? Is something wrong?"

"No, nothing...it's just that Inigo is so young!" Magdalena burst out. "I worry about him more than your other children. He seems to want to grow up too quickly..."

"Now, Magdalena," Don Beltrán gently chided, "it will be good for Inigo to spend some time away from home. He'll never mature if he stays here. After all, the boy is sixteen. Juan Velázquez will help him grow into a fine man. And what's more, he'll be trained as a soldier. One day he'll be given a good position as an officer of rank. You know that's what he's always wanted."

"Yes, but all Inigo sees is the glamor of war. He knows nothing of the hardships to be faced…"

"That's because we've sheltered and pampered him all his life," Don Beltrán interrupted. "We must encourage and support him now that he's accepted the offer to live at court. You'll see, Magdalena, it will be for the best."

Magdalena sighed and nodded. "I suppose you're right. But I'll miss him."

"I will too," Don Beltrán quietly admitted.

❖ ❖ ❖

There were days of anxious waiting until a carriage finally arrived from the Velázquez castle. Inigo loaded his belongings and said a tearful goodbye to the family.

"God be with you," Magdalena whispered as she embraced him.

"Be sure to write," his brother Martín reminded.

Don Beltrán grasped Inigo firmly by the shoulders.

*"I'll make you proud, Father, you and
the entire House of Loyola."*

"Goodbye, Father," Inigo murmured. "I'll try my hardest to make you proud of me—you and the entire House of Loyola."

"I know you will," Don Beltrán answered in a husky voice.

Swallowing the lump in his own throat, Inigo swung open the door of the carriage and jumped in. The coachman shut it behind him. In a moment they were off. Inigo leaned out the window and waved until a curve in the road blocked his view.

What adventures lay ahead of him?

He wondered.

3

A SOLDIER AT LAST

Beltrán de Loyola died suddenly a year after Inigo left home. Inigo then became almost like an adopted son of Don Juan Velázquez.

He spent ten years at the Velázquez castle, and was recognized as one of the finest pages in the area. Under the direction of tutors, Inigo learned all the customs and manners necessary to be of service at official functions.

These were happy years for young Inigo. He no longer went to school because he was too busy learning to be a "gentleman of the court." Instead he attended to knights and ladies who visited the castle. He listened to the thrilling stories they told around the hearth at night.

Señor Velázquez had an immense library and gave Inigo permission to use it during his free moments. There, Inigo buried himself in one adventure novel and romance after another. Daydreaming was still one of his favorite pastimes!

Shortly after Inigo turned twenty-six, Señor Velázquez died. Inigo was deeply saddened and deeply felt the loss. He stayed on at the castle for several months in order to be of service to Señora Velázquez. But soon he grew restless. One day he saddled a horse and rode to the home of Don Anthony Manrique, the Duke of Nájera, who was also a close relative of his.

"Inigo!" the duke greeted him warmly. "Tell me, to what do I owe this unexpected visit? I haven't seen you for years. How are you?"

"Very well, my lord," Inigo started out. "I've come to ask you a favor."

"Granted," the nobleman replied. "Just tell me what it is."

"I've desired for a long time to join the king's army. I'm not trained in the use of military arms, but if you allow me to enter your service, I promise to give you my best and learn all that I am taught."

The duke looked thoughtfully at the young man for a moment. He remembered Beltrán's desire to have a son in the king's army. Perhaps it was time….

"Inigo, military life is difficult. The war between Spain and France is real. Men fight and die on both sides. Do you know what you're asking?"

"Yes, my lord." Inigo answered confidently.

This is not the young Inigo I remember, the duke thought. *He has gained a real maturity.* The duke smiled reassuringly. "Welcome, Don Inigo," he said as he held out his hand. "We shall begin the training tomorrow!"

❖   ❖   ❖

Inigo threw himself into the study of the weapons and military tactics of his day. Strategy became his strong point, and in no time at all he proved himself capable of taking charge of any situation. There was an air of command about him that made other knights rally around him for direction and advice. He passionately loved military life and willingly sacrificed any comfort or convenience in order to be a better soldier.

After four short years, Inigo achieved the rank of captain and was placed in command of his own company of soldiers. In May of 1521, Captain Inigo de Loyola and his company received orders to defend the fortress of Pamplona, Spain. France's invading troops had heavily attacked the small fort, and it was on the verge of falling into the hands of the enemy.

Inigo had no way of knowing that this battle was to change his life....

4

Bitter Defeat

"You, there!" Inigo shouted to a soldier hurrying past. "Help load the cannon!" Inigo struggled to ignore the weariness he felt. The fort had been under bombardment for six grueling hours, and still the French were pouring in with fresh troops. How could he and his men hold out?

The air was thick with smoke. Deafening cannon blasts drew closer. From all directions cannonballs came ripping through the walls of the fortress, wounding some Spaniards and killing others.

Inigo's troops began to panic. "We're lost!" wailed one of the men. "The French are already at the wall! We must run..."

"Yes! Run!" other voices shouted.

"No! Stay at your posts!" Inigo bellowed. "We must not lose Pamplona! We must hold on for Spain!" Inigo's eyes were blazing as he raced toward the breach in the wall. "I'll *never* give up!" he cried. "It's better to die as brave men than to save ourselves through cowardice!"

Suddenly a loud explosion erupted. A cannonball came tearing through a break in the thick wall. It struck Inigo, shattering his right leg. As the ball ricocheted off the opposite wall, flying pieces of stone badly gashed his other leg. Thrown to the ground, Inigo lay bleeding. A hot, searing pain shot through his legs. Then…there was nothing.

❖　❖　❖

Everything was dim and blurry. "Where …where am I?" Inigo moaned.

As he struggled to raise his head, he became conscious of a sharp, aching pain in his legs. He closed his eyes and fell back on the pillow.

"Captain," said one of his men, "this is a French hospital."

"Pamplona?" Inigo whispered.

"We've lost Pamplona, but the French have treated us with kindness, caring for our wounded and sick."

"My legs!" Inigo groaned.

"Your legs have been saved by the French doctors," the Spanish soldier replied.

"They are set and bandaged, Captain. You've been treated with the greatest respect. Your bravery has inspired everyone."

During those first days of recovery Inigo wandered in and out of delirium, talking about Pamplona and calling his men to battle. "My men, why have they fallen?" he cried in his feverish sleep. "My legs...my legs.... Pamplona has fallen!"

After about two weeks, when he was strong enough to be moved, the French decided to send Inigo home with honor. He was still unable to walk, so they assigned men to bear him back to Loyola on a stretcher. It was a long journey on foot. It was also extremely painful for Inigo, since his bones hadn't healed and the mountain roads were rough and bumpy. Greater than any physical pain, however, was the bitterness of failure and defeat.

Many of my comrades died.... and why? Inigo thought. *Because of my mistakes? What did Spain and France hope to achieve from this war? So many men lost on both sides. And for what?*

Inigo fought the battle of Pamplona again in his mind as the stretcher-bearers approached the Loyola castle. Finally they arrived. Inigo's brother Martín was away, but his sister-in-law Magdalena welcomed him warmly.

"Inigo! Thank God you're home again!" she exclaimed as he was carried in.

Inigo smiled weakly and tried to sit up. "I'm happy to be home."

"It's good that you've come to rest," Magdalena continued soothingly.

"Rest?" Inigo seemed disturbed. "Not to rest! I must recover and return to my post. Spain needs me."

"Of course, Inigo, of course," Magdalena agreed. "You'll certainly recover soon. We'll take you to your room, now. You must be tired after such a long trip."

5

AN IRON WILL

Contrary to his hopes, Inigo's recovery was slow. When Martín returned home, he and Magdalena decided to call in the best physicians and surgeons. But the diagnosis wasn't encouraging: "The bones of his right leg have been set improperly and have bonded. Because of this, Señor de Loyola will be left with a slight limp."

A slight limp! Inigo was stunned. "Do you mean I'll be deformed for life?" he demanded.

"Not deformed. At least not visibly so," one of the doctors kindly explained. "You are already quite fortunate to have survived such a blow, Señor, and the French doctors did the best they could under the circumstances. You are young, and will soon be leading a normal life once again. It will not be possible, however, to return to a military career."

"What do you mean it won't be possible!" Inigo shouted. "There must be something you can do! I can't spend the rest of my life a...a...cripple! I won't! Surely your medical knowledge..."

"Señor de Loyola," the doctor interrupted with a grim look on his face, "the only way to straighten your leg is to break the bone again and reset it correctly. I must warn you, the pain will be excruciating, and though you might come through the operation, there is no guarantee of success. I can only try. In my opinion..."

"Your opinion isn't necessary," Inigo cut in. "I will undergo the operation as soon as you're ready to perform it."

❖   ❖   ❖

Magdalena wrung the water from the cool cloth and gently laid it upon Inigo's burning forehead. Her lips moved in silent prayer. *If only the fever would break!* It had been days now since the operation, and Inigo seemed to be worsening. He had remained completely conscious throughout the brutal surgery—a surgery that had been performed without anesthetics. The pain had been unbearable. With his iron will Inigo had clenched his fists, but had never spoken or cried out. Now he was no longer eating, and the doctors had given up all hope for his recovery.

"I tried to tell him," the surgeon said with a sad shake of his head.

"We all tried, Doctor. He's in God's hands now," Martín replied.

Magdalena had stayed by Inigo's side day and night, caring for him as she would have cared for her own brother. She looked up as Martín and the doctor started to leave the room.

"What day is this, Martín?" she asked softly.

"June 28, the eve of the feast of Saints Peter and Paul."

Magdalena pulled her chair closer to Inigo's bed. *Inigo has always been very devoted to Saint Peter,* she thought. *I remember hearing that once he even wrote a poem in the apostle's honor. Holy Apostles Peter and Paul,* she suddenly found herself praying, *you could obtain from God a cure for Inigo.*

She reached into her pocket and drew out her rosary. It was already very late. Her eyes were heavy with sorrow and lack of sleep, but she would stay with Inigo as she had last night and the night before. She hadn't finished praying the first mystery when her eyes closed and the rosary slipped into her lap.

When Magdalena awoke, the room was flooded with the morning sun. *It's morning already?* she thought with a start.

"I've been waiting for you to wake up, Magdalena," came a familiar voice from the bed. "You're late, and I'm hungry. I need something to eat!"

"Inigo!"

There he lay, eyes wide open, with a grin spread over his face and the cloth that had covered his forehead tossed to one side.

"Inigo! I...you.... It's a miracle! Blessed be God!" Magdalena half whispered. "I'll get Martín right away!"

"And don't forget the breakfast," Inigo called after her.

6
CONVERSION

As Inigo's leg began to heal again, a complication set in. One bone overlapped the other, causing an ugly bulge just below the knee. This made his right leg shorter than his left. Not only did Inigo now have a *real* physical deformity, but he would certainly limp. His pride couldn't take this. "Operate again!" he ordered the surgeon. "Cut away the bone! Do whatever you must to stretch the leg!"

Again Inigo went through an unbelievably painful operation, fully conscious and without a moan.

The weeks dragged on while his leg slowly healed. Being confined to bed while the summer days slipped by was an added torment for him. He longed for the days he had known—days full of excitement and adventure. The stifling heat didn't help matters either. Sometimes even a small breeze felt like a blast of fire. It was all so frustrating.

"Magdalena!" Inigo called sharply. "Magdalena!"

His sister-in-law came running. "What is it, Inigo? Has something happened?"

"I wish something *would* happen...I'm terribly bored. Could you please bring me some novels? I feel like reading. Make it something exciting, now."

Inigo didn't know that when Martín and Magdalena had married, they had removed all novels from the house.

"Of course, Inigo," Magdalena smilingly replied. "I'll get you something right away."

She returned almost immediately carrying two large volumes.

"Ah, excellent," Inigo approved.

Ignoring his comment, Magdalena placed the books on the table beside his bed. "I'm sorry, Inigo," she apologized, "but these are all I could find. I must go now, but I'll be back shortly. I'm sure these stories will keep you well occupied."

With that she turned and quickly left the room.

Inigo eagerly picked up one book and read *The Life of Christ*. "What's this?" he muttered. He reached for the second. Stamped on its cover was the title *Lives of the Saints*.

"Magdalena!" Inigo growled, waving the book at the closed door, "I want no part of this!"

"Magdalena!" Inigo growled.
"I want no part of this!"

But his sister-in-law was well out of earshot. Martín caught her running down the hall.

"Magdalena, what's the matter?" he asked in surprise.

"I just gave Inigo two books to read...*The Life of Christ* and the *Lives of the Saints,*" she breathlessly explained. "I don't think he's very satisfied with my choice."

"I think your choice was excellent," her husband chuckled. "If he has a complaint, tell him to call me."

The minutes ticked by. Inigo *was* bored. He couldn't get out of bed, and the two titles were the only books in the room. Reluctantly he picked up the *Lives of the Saints.* The chapters were fairly short. Inigo leafed through the thick volume and came across the story of Saint Francis. He read it and moved on to Saint Dominic. He soon found that he couldn't put the book down!

Magdalena returned much later and quietly opened the door. Inigo was so absorbed in reading that he didn't notice her. Without a sound, she closed the door again and tiptoed off to find Martín.

"How is my impetuous little brother?" he asked.

"He's reading the *Lives of the Saints* and didn't even notice me when I looked in on him. I think that someday he will be as gentle and kind as you, my husband."

"Perhaps better, Magdalena. Perhaps better."

Inigo continued to read even as it grew dark outside. He strained to pick out the words. It wasn't that he *enjoyed* what he was reading, he told himself. It was as if he *had* to read ahead—as if something inside him were forcing him to continue.

When Magdalena returned with supper, Inigo was strangely quiet.

"Will you bring me a candle to read by?" he asked.

"Of course. Do you need anything else?"

"No, thank you, Magdalena. Just the candle and I'll be fine for the evening."

The candle finally burned itself out and Inigo set the book on the table. Slipping back under the covers, he tried to sleep. But his thoughts made rest impossible. *The men and women in that book were real people, true heroes and heroines. They had exceptional courage and sometimes even gave up their lives. And for what? They sought no honor or glory for themselves....*

Inigo turned on his side. Moonlight streaming through the open window fell on the second book—*The Life of Christ.* Somehow he knew that it contained the answers he was searching for.

❖   ❖   ❖

"Inigo, you've been on your crutches all morning. You'd better rest now," advised Martín.

His brother nodded and sank into a near-by chair. Since he had been able to get out of bed and walk, Inigo had been exerting himself to the point of exhaustion. He still couldn't accept the fact that his career as a soldier was over. His mind was full of questions. *Is it really military life that makes me happy? Am I content to lead the life I was living before, when I think of the saints who gave everything to God? Surely I can be like them…. Can I do any less?*

Inigo was confused and uncertain. He wanted to return to his former life, yet he also wanted to serve God with all his heart.

Even though his leg throbbed with pain, he raised himself from the chair and made his way to a painting of the Blessed Virgin.

With great effort he knelt before the Madonna, begging for her help. He was troubled by haunting thoughts as he hobbled back to his room. *Whenever I dream of glory and fame, I feel so empty inside. It's as if something is missing from my life. But when I read about Jesus and the saints who followed him, I'm filled with a peace and happiness I've never felt before. Maybe these thoughts are from God. If so, I must follow Jesus! If Francis and Dominic could become saints, why can't I?*

That night Inigo had a wonderful experience. While he was lying awake in the dark, he saw the Mother of God holding the Child Jesus in her arms. She looked at Inigo with great kindness and smiled at him. Inigo knew from then on that Mary would be his special guide, leading him to Jesus.

One of his greatest consolations during the long and painful period of his recuperation was to gaze at the stars. He would do this for hours, feeling a strange and new attraction to serve the Lord. "How dim the earth seems when I lift my eyes to heaven!" he would repeat again and again.

7

THE PILGRIM

"Can't you visit the Duke of Nájera once you're stronger?" Magdalena pleaded.

"I've already made arrangements," Inigo replied with a shake of his head. "I can't go back on my word. He's expecting me. Besides, the journey will do me good."

"Inigo," Martín broke in firmly, "please listen to reason. You've been acting so strange lately. It's as if you're another person."

"Nonsense! It's my duty to make a report to the duke now that I've recovered. After all, he is still my commanding officer. I'll take every precaution. I promise."

"If there's no changing your mind, we'll have to let you go," Martín sighed. "But it's not without concern."

"I'll be leaving early tomorrow morning, so I should say goodbye."

The brothers shook hands warmly.

"God be with you," Magdalena said.

Inigo leaned over and kissed her on the cheek. "I'm grateful for all you've done for me, Magdalena. Believe me when I say that

I owe my present happiness to you." Inigo bowed graciously and left the room.

Martín watched his brother limp up the stairs. Turning, he saw Magdalena brush away a tear.

"Don't worry," he said gently, "I'm sending two servants with Inigo. They'll bring him home safely."

Magdalena nodded. She couldn't explain it, but somehow she knew that Inigo wouldn't be coming back.

❖   ❖   ❖

Inigo made his promised report to the duke. He followed it with his statement of resignation from military service. The duke tried every argument to convince him to remain in the army, but all failed. Once Inigo had made up his mind, it was difficult to change it!

The next shock was dealt to Martín's two servants. "Return home without me," Inigo ordered them.

"But where are you going, Señor de Loyola, and what shall we tell your brother?"

"Tell Martín that I'm going wherever God wills me to go. I've chosen the road to holiness and that's the one I will follow. Give my love to everyone. I promise to bring honor to the name of Loyola."

With those words Inigo reined his mule toward the road that led to the mountain of Montserrat. His plan was to go as a pilgrim to the Benedictine monastery there and spend time in prayer.

As he rode up the mountainside, Inigo felt a new thrill and excitement. *I've taken the first step and left all that the world has to offer me. I'm choosing to follow the King of kings. I want nothing more than to follow Jesus, to become a pilgrim and visit the places where he lived and walked on this earth.*

As he prayed and thought, he came up to another man riding on a mule.

"Where are you headed?" the stranger asked.

"To Montserrat, to make a pilgrimage and to pray at the monastery," Inigo answered pleasantly.

The man was not a Spaniard, and as they briefly spoke, Inigo discovered that neither was he a Christian.

When Inigo brought up the topic of the Virgin Mary, he found that the stranger did not share his beliefs concerning the Mother of God. On the contrary, the man spoke against some of the Church's teachings on Mary. Inigo began to argue his point. Seeing his temper begin to flare, the foreigner decided that it was time to leave. He spurred his mule and rode off, leaving Inigo in a cloud of dust.

I should defend our Lady's honor! I should go after him and teach him a lesson he'll never forget! Inigo fumed as he rode on. As he struggled to control his anger, another voice inside him gently urged: *That man is your brother. Jesus loves him, too. Because he is not a Christian, can you hold it against him?*

The road suddenly forked before him. One path led to Montserrat, the other was the way taken by the stranger. Inigo halted. *Oh Lord,* he prayed, *I have given you my life. Do with me as you please. Decide, then, whether I should punish the man who has insulted your holy Mother, or go on my way to Montserrat.*

Inigo relaxed his grip on the reins. Left to itself, his mule veered to the left and took the road leading to Montserrat and the Benedictine abbey.

So be it, Lord. Your will be done, Inigo prayed in his heart. *Lead me where you will.*

By the time Inigo reached the monastery on Saturday, March 21, 1522, he was tired, cold, and dusty. His injured leg pounded with pain. But he felt a deep inner peace and happiness.

He approached the large iron gate and rang the bell. An elderly monk soon appeared. If he was surprised to find an elegantly dressed soldier with a bandaged leg, he didn't show it. "Welcome," the monk said kindly as he opened the gate.

"Brother, I am a pilgrim," Inigo explained, "and have come to visit the shrine. I would like to spend time in prayer before the Mother of God and beg the Lord's forgiveness for the sins of my past life. I also wish to confess my sins. I have stumbled and fallen, but I want to rise again."

"You are most welcome here," the monk replied. "Stay as long as you wish. Come, I will take you to the chapel of Our Lady of Montserrat."

After speaking with a monk named Don Juan Chanon about the confession he desired to make, Inigo was given a room at the monastery. An eyewitness later reported that during his three days there Inigo fasted on bread and water, confessed all the sins of his past life, and could constantly "be seen in front of the altar of our Lady, weeping."

The soldier who had once had a passion for reading novels about knights and chivalry confided to Don Juan after his confession, "Now I want to become a knight of God."

At that time there were prescribed ceremonies for becoming a knight. Inigo knew them well. He knew that besides going to confession, an all-night prayer vigil followed by Mass and Holy Communion were required. It was also the custom to bring to the vigil the arms a knight would bear in battle.

Inigo chose the night of March 24, the eve of the feast of the Annunciation, for his vigil. That night he secretly gave away his expensive clothing to a poor man and donned a sackcloth robe, rope belt and rope sandals. He returned to our Lady's chapel and spent the whole night praying before the altar. Sometimes he knelt, sometimes he stood, leaning against his pilgrim's staff when the pain in his wounded leg became too great. But he never sat. *Mother of God,* he prayed, *from this moment on I promise to live only for you and for your Son. Everything I loved before means nothing to me now. I will be a soldier for Jesus, the King of kings. I will bring honor to his name by teaching others to love him.*

Inigo had also arranged for Don Juan to lay his engraved sword and jeweled dagger on the altar. Later, these would be displayed with other objects pilgrims had left as offerings to the Lord and the Blessed Virgin.

At dawn the monastery's gate opened again. The proud Captain de Loyola was no more. It was a humbly dressed beggar who walked away in his place.

8

MANRESA

In the months that followed, Inigo spent most of his time serving the poor and the sick at the hospital of Santa Lucia in the town of Manresa. He washed their sores, dressed them with ointments, and comforted the lepers and those with incurable diseases. The joy he knew mounted with every passing day.

Daily Inigo walked from house to house to beg his food from the townspeople. They soon came to know and love the humble stranger who often prayed in a nearby cave. The Dominican priests of Manresa even gave him a room at their monastery. Inigo spent many hours in prayer, fasting, and penance. He was sorry for all his sins and wanted to prove this to God by going against his own will. The people of Manresa began to talk among themselves.

"This pilgrim is different," one old man observed. "He doesn't seem at all concerned about his appearance. He lets his hair and fingernails grow. He wears one sandal on his right foot, while the other foot is bare."

"The children laugh at him," a woman added. "They call him 'Old Man Sack,' because of that rough robe he wears. But he laughs right along with them, and doesn't seem offended. The children love him. They run after him to the church steps where he sits and teaches them their catechism. I've never seen anything like it!"

But during his stay in Manresa Inigo performed so many penances that he weakened his body and began to experience doubts and temptations. *What if God hasn't really forgiven me? What if I forgot to mention all my sins to the priest when I went to confession? What if all my good works are useless?* Torturous thoughts like these played themselves over and over again in his mind. He became very discouraged and began to lose hope. Weakened by all his fasting and penance, Inigo also became seriously ill. At different times the townspeople took him into their homes and cared for him.

Finally, after much prayer, Inigo began to understand that God's love and mercy are *greater* than any sin we can ever commit. He realized that God *always* forgives us when we're sorry. God allowed him to see that his worries were really temptations from the devil, who was trying to stop him from doing good.

One day while he was praying on the bank of the Cardoner River, Inigo received a special light from God. God instantly let him understand and know many things—about prayer, about faith, and even about human wisdom. The Lord then gave him the inspiration to found a group of men who would dedicate their entire lives to Jesus and his Church. Inigo later revealed that all the blessings he received during his entire life were less than those he received that day by the river.

During his time at Manresa Inigo also wrote down reflections which he called the *Spiritual Exercises*. These were experiences Inigo underwent in his spiritual journey toward God. He wrote them in the cave on the outskirts of the town. Later on, the *Spiritual Exercises* would lead many people closer to God.

Inigo didn't write the *Exercises* all at once. They were written a little at a time, as he himself learned and practiced the spiritual life.

The *Spiritual Exercises* are designed to help one know oneself better. They include instructions on how to examine oneself, meditate on the life of Jesus, and pray so that one can imitate Jesus more closely.

The winter of 1522 was very difficult for Inigo, and he fell ill once again. This time the Ferrera family took him in and cared for him. After he recovered, some of the noble ladies of the town insisted that he begin to dress properly, wearing shoes and a hat. They sewed him two dark jackets made of a heavy woven cloth, and a cap of the same material.

Now Inigo felt it was time to move on.

9

BACK TO SCHOOL

After leaving Manresa, Inigo traveled to Barcelona. From there he set out on a pilgrimage to Rome, arriving there on Palm Sunday, 1523. But his real goal was the Holy Land. Journeying on to Venice from Rome, Inigo found a ship that agreed to give him free passage to Jerusalem. For five weeks Inigo walked in the footsteps of Jesus and visited all the holy places and shrines. His dream was to live out the rest of his life in Jerusalem. But the Franciscans whom the Pope had put in charge of the Holy Land told him this wasn't possible and refused him permission. "It's just too dangerous," the Franciscan superior insisted. "Other pilgrims who have tried to stay have been kidnapped by the Turks. Some have been imprisoned, some even killed."

Disappointed, Inigo sailed back to Venice with the rest of the pilgrims. Now what was he to do? He felt strongly called to bring others closer to God. But he realized that to be effective he would need more of an education. He decided to go back to Barcelona—and school.

❖ ❖ ❖

"*What* did you say?" asked the dazed schoolmaster.

"I'd like to be admitted to your Latin class," came the quiet reply.

Jeronimo Ardévol blinked in amazement. The stranger before him was of medium height and slight build. Ardévol would later learn that he was thirty-three years old. There was an air of nobility about him, although he was dressed like a beggar. The teacher tried not to stare at the sackcloth robe the man wore, nor at the piece of rope he used for a belt. Looking down didn't help because there his eyes met calloused feet resting on thin, rope sandals. The schoolmaster forced himself to meet the penetrating gaze of the stranger. Under normal circumstances, Master Ardévol would have laughed at a grown man asking to be admitted to a children's class. But there was something very different about *this* man.

"Who are you?" Ardévol asked.

"Do you realize that I only teach children here?"

"My name is Inigo de Loyola. I have received very little education and now I'd like to further my studies."

"Do you realize that I only teach children here? Surely you don't want to enroll in a course with young boys. The students would laugh you out of the classroom!"

"Perhaps I should explain," Inigo calmly replied. "For some years now I have devoted my life to the service of God. I have spoken about God and his goodness, and tried to help others find him as I have found him. My greatest desire was to travel to Jerusalem and make Christianity known there. I did go, but I was not permitted to stay. I know that God has given me a mission and that I am to help many persons come to him and his Church. But it has been made clear to me that to serve him better, to combat heresies and errors rising against his Church, I need more studies. And so," Inigo concluded with a smile, "I've come to Barcelona. I'm prepared to start from the very beginning, with Latin grammar."

The schoolmaster was thoughtful for some time. "I admire your will to learn," he finally said in a respectful tone. "Not many men are prepared to sacrifice their pride in such a way. You will be welcome in my class."

10

TROUBLES

Inigo studied under Master Ardévol for two years and learned enough Latin to begin a philosophy course at the University of Alcala. He attended classes there for about a year and a half. He also continued to speak about God and prayer to anyone who would listen.

This was a time when certain religious errors were being spread, and many in the Church were cautious and overly fearful of anyone who "preached." It was also the time of the Spanish Inquisition. The Inquisition was a type of court that had been set up by King Ferdinand and Queen Isabella of Spain in 1479. Its members included both civil and Church authorities, and its purpose was to seek out and punish heretics, or persons who had been accused of spreading false teachings about the Catholic faith. The Spanish Inquisition also searched out Jews and Muslims who had converted to Christianity, but who still secretly practiced their own religion.

In such an atmosphere of fear and suspicion, many abuses developed, and the Inquisitors or judges of the Inquisition were often cruel in their treatment of suspected heretics. Inigo ended up being arrested by some Inquisitors in Alcala because a man had wrongly reported that Inigo had convinced a noblewoman and her daughter to go on a pilgrimage! He was held in prison for over a month until the women returned home and cleared him of the charges. "Now you are forbidden to instruct people in the faith for four years," the officials told Inigo upon his release.

The Church authorities felt he needed more education in order to preach. Inigo agreed. He decided to pursue his studies at the University of Salamanca, the most famous of the Spanish schools. But at Salamanca he again found himself in trouble with the Inquisition....

Some curious Dominican priests invited him to supper. The meal was followed by a kind of interrogation by the vice-superior. "Where have you studied? *What* have you studied? What do you preach? Have you received special revelations from the Holy Spirit?"

Sensing that he might be misunderstood, Inigo simply responded, "Father, I will say no more than what I've already said."

"We have our ways of making you talk!" the Dominicans retorted. And with that, they locked Inigo, and a companion who was with him, in the Dominican chapel! After three days the two were taken to the Salamanca prison. Three weeks later they were finally released.

"We find no fault with your teaching," the Inquisitors told them, "but from now on, you're not allowed to teach people about what is a venial sin and what is a mortal sin."

Inigo had barely been in Salamanca two months, and had spent a good part of that time in prison. Since he couldn't speak about sin in Salamanca, he decided to move on to Paris. There he hoped to finally complete his studies. But before leaving for Paris, Inigo returned to Barcelona, where he begged for the money he would need to pay his tuition.

The distance from Barcelona, Spain, to Paris, France, was about five hundred miles. Inigo walked them alone. He stopped along the way, begging his food or lodging for the night. Sometimes he slept out in the open under a tree. It was winter. The air was harsh and the ground was frozen. But Inigo was happy to resemble Jesus, who so often had had nowhere to lay his head.

"Oh, Lord," Inigo would pray, "you have been too good to me!" Looking up at the stars he would think, *How unattractive the world seems when I look toward heaven.*

It was February 1528 when he reached Paris. Inigo was thirty-seven years old. He enrolled at the university under the name he had used in his Latin class and by which he would be known from then on—Ignatius de Loyola.

11

ROOMMATES

"Welcome, Ignatius! My name is Peter... Peter Favre. I've heard a lot about you. I've been wanting to meet you for some time."

"I've also heard many good things about you," Ignatius replied with a friendly shake of the younger man's hand. "Father Peña has highly recommended you. I'm grateful to you for agreeing to tutor me, besides letting me share your room."

The twenty-three-year-old Frenchman smiled. He felt completely at ease with this soft-spoken Spaniard.

"Do you know that you're quite a controversial figure here, Ignatius? Everyone's been talking about you since the moment you set foot on campus."

"Is that so?" Ignatius answered in amusement. "And what could they possibly say about a poor beggar from Spain?"

"Some say you're crazy to continue your education so late in life. Others say you have strange ideas regarding the faith. Then there are those who believe you are truly a holy and wise man."

"And what do you think?"

"I think that one should never stop learning his whole life long because the more one learns, the more one honors God who gave us our mind in the first place."

Ignatius nodded and smiled.

"Why don't we go up to our room now, before Francis gets back," Peter suggested a little nervously.

"Francis?"

"Yes. Francis Xavier. He shares the room too. He's also a Spaniard. From a city called Navarre, I believe. Do you know the place?"

"I know it well."

❖ ❖ ❖

"Peter! Are you out of your mind?" exploded the fiery Francis in exasperation. "You actually invited this beggar to come and live with us?"

"Francis, that's not fair," Peter protested quietly. "Ignatius isn't a beggar, and besides, Father Peña suggested that he room with us, and that I help him with his studies. He really didn't have a place to stay."

"He didn't have a place to stay," Francis dully echoed. "I suppose you offered him my bed, too!"

"No, but do you happen to have an extra blanket?"

"That's it! This is too…"

A knock at the door interrupted the heated conversation.

"Come in!" yelled Francis sharply, turning to see the cause of his anger standing in the doorway.

"Ignatius!" Peter brushed past Francis. "Ignatius, come in and meet Francis Xavier."

Peter introduced the two, ignoring Francis' smoldering dark eyes.

"It's very kind of you to allow me to stay here. I hope I won't be too much of an inconvenience," Ignatius said quietly.

There was dead silence as two pairs of eyes leveled their gaze on Francis.

"Sure…. It won't be any problem at all," Francis mumbled awkwardly. He suddenly sprinted for the door, calling over his shoulder, "I have to go out. I'll be back tonight." Just before he slammed it shut, he added, "The blanket's in the wardrobe."

"Francis is a good friend of mine, Ignatius. He'll be fine once he calms down. He has a hot temper, you know, but it doesn't last. He loves sports and is one of our best runners. He always wins."

Ignatius didn't seem to be listening. He was looking past the door with a thoughtful expression on his face.

Strange, Peter thought, *it's almost as if he already* knows *Francis.*

12

DISCIPLES

In the days that followed, Ignatius and Peter became inseparable friends—they studied together, ate together, and had long talks about spiritual matters.

Peter had been experiencing some temptations against his faith and was confused about his future. But when he listened to Ignatius, he understood things more clearly and became surer and surer of what he wanted to do with his life.

"Ignatius," Peter confided to him one day, "I feel I'm being called by God. I want to follow this call, but sometimes I find it so hard and I'm afraid that I'm unworthy..."

"Unworthy?"

"Unworthy to become a priest," Peter blurted out. "I want to become a priest."

A warm smile spread over Ignatius's face.

"You've known all along, haven't you, Ignatius? Why didn't you tell me?"

"That you have a vocation to the priesthood?" Ignatius's smile grew wider. "I've never stopped praying that you would recognize and accept the gift God has entrusted to you."

"Ignatius, I've often heard you speak about the *Spiritual Exercises*. Do you think I'm ready to make them?"

"Yes," Ignatius agreed. "You're ready."

❖   ❖   ❖

Francis Xavier scowled as he climbed the stairs to the dormitory. Usually, after eating out in the evenings, he *stayed* out as long as he could. It wasn't only because he liked having a good time. The main reason was that he knew the "group" would be meeting in the dorm. Other students interested in what Ignatius had to say had started getting together in the evenings to listen to him and to discuss spiritual matters.

Francis's mind was racing. *They'll all be there, waiting for Ignatius. He's already got Peter convinced that he should become a priest. Well, not me! Let the others run after him if they want to. I have more important plans. I think I've made that plain to him. The trouble is that he doesn't listen! I don't* want *his life of poverty, humility, and complete dedication to God!*

He had one more stairway to climb, but his thoughts pushed on. *And then there's his infuriating question: "Francis, 'what does it profit a man who gains the whole world but suffers the loss of his soul?'" I try to lead a good life. What more could God possibly want?*

Deep down, Francis knew. But he didn't want to admit it. *Why should I give up everything—a career, success, a happy life—to join a band of beggars? It's fine for them, but not for me. I could never be like them.*

With a sigh, Francis quietly pushed open the door to his room.

He was surprised to see Ignatius sitting alone at the table, studying. Ignatius didn't look up as Francis entered. For a moment the younger man found himself in an awkward position. He wasn't quite sure what to do. He felt a sudden urge to speak to Ignatius, but he didn't know where to begin.

Ignatius himself broke the silence. "What's bothering you, Francis?"

The next thing he knew, Francis was sitting by Ignatius pouring out every question, argument, doubt and anxiety that was troubling his mind and heart.

Ignatius listened patiently. "Are you trying to convince me or yourself?" he asked when Francis finished.

Francis was startled.

"If we expect no other life than the one we live on earth—and we are born only to die—if there really is no heaven, then you are the wise one, and I'm the fool," Ignatius went on calmly. "On the other hand, if there *is* a heaven which awaits us, you're giving up eternal happiness for a world of temporary joys and pleasures. That's very foolish, wouldn't you say? Think of it, Francis: if you want to reach heaven, who can stop you? All that the world has to offer is still not enough to satisfy your soul or fill the emptiness of your heart. Only God can do that."

Francis stared at Ignatius, whose face seemed to grow more and more radiant as he spoke.

"The choice is yours, Francis. No one can make it for you. Everything is up to you."

Hours after his conversation with Ignatius, Francis was still praying. He felt peaceful and sure now. *You want me, Lord,* he prayed, *and how much I do want you. I will follow Ignatius— to you.*

HUMBLE BEGINNINGS

It was the feast of the Assumption, August 15, 1534. The sun had not yet risen as seven men knelt in prayer in the Chapel of Saint Denis on the hill of Montmartre.

The simple altar before them was set for Mass, candles flickering in the semi-darkness. A silver bell tinkled. Ignatius de Loyola, Francis Xavier, Simon Rodriguez, Diego Laynez, Alfonso Salmeron and Nicolas Bobadilla stood as the priest emerged and reverently kissed the altar. It was Father Peter Favre.

All of these companions of Ignatius had gone through the Spiritual Exercises and had decided to follow him in his new way of life. They banded together inspired by the same ideal and the same goal: All for the greater glory of God.

Just before Communion, each man made a vow of chastity and poverty, together with a promise to make a pilgrimage to the Holy Land and to work for the spread of Christianity there. While they were not yet an official religious order—that would come later—they were in a special way consecrating their lives to God.

In the months that followed, members of the group completed their studies at the University of Paris. They next moved on to Venice, Italy, where they spent much of their time caring for the poor and sick in the city's hospitals. Many, especially the incurable patients, had been abandoned by family and friends. Their loneliness, suffering and pain led them to the brink of despair, but Ignatius and his band of men brought new hope as they washed and bandaged wounds, offering these men and women words of comfort and faith. The love and dedication of Ignatius and his friends slowly brought about a transformation within the hospital itself.

❖   ❖   ❖

While his little community sat eating supper one evening, Ignatius made an announcement: "Now is the time to make our pilgrimage to the Holy Land."

His companions happily slapped their hands on the table as a sign of their enthusiastic agreement.

"The pilgrim ships usually set sail in July, and it's already March," one of the young men observed.

"Yes," Ignatius replied, "we'll have to work quickly. I'd like to send you to Rome to obtain the Pope's blessing for our pilgrimage...," he paused and looked around the table, "and ask his permission to be ordained priests."

Pope Paul III blessed their pilgrimage and granted them permission to be ordained priests by a bishop of their own choosing. The six excitedly returned to Venice with the good news. On June 24, 1537, all except Peter Favre, who was already a priest, and Alfonso Salmeron, who was still too young, were ordained priests by Bishop Nigusanti of Arbe.

By July, they had packed their few belongings and made their way to the Venetian port where the pilgrim ships were docked. They were anxious to set out for Jerusalem.

"I WILL HELP YOU IN ROME"

"Absolutely not! It's out of the question!" yelled the captain, slamming his chubby fist down on his desk. "Are you the only ones who haven't heard about the war with the Turks? No pilgrim ships are allowed to leave the harbor. And certainly not mine! My vessel will sail elsewhere!"

"Perhaps it will sail nowhere," Ignatius quietly replied.

The captain glared but made no comment. Ignatius and his friends turned and left. A few days later, that very ship sunk within sight of the shore as it sailed from the harbor to join the fighting.

The threat of war between Venice and Turkey had been pending for some time. Minor skirmishes flared with Turkish ships in the Sea of Ionia, but now a full-fledged battle had broken out and passage to the Holy Land was impossible for the time being.

"What will we do now, Father Ignatius?" his followers asked.

"We'll spread out to other cities. We'll preach, teach, and work in the hospitals just as we've done here in Venice. I'll go to Rome with Father Peter and Father Diego, since the Holy Father has sent us a letter requesting us to visit him. The rest of you will go to Padua, Siena and Bologna for now."

❖   ❖   ❖

"Father Ignatius, why don't we stop and rest? We've been traveling since early morning. You must be tired."

Ignatius turned and looked at Father Diego. "Tired? No, Diego, I was just thinking.... We're getting close to La Storta. Isn't there a chapel there, just off the main road?"

"Yes, I believe there is. We could easily stop there if you'd like."

The three dusty travelers soon came upon the chapel at the fork in the road. There they knelt in prayer for a long time.

Ignatius gazed at the tabernacle, immersed in conversation with the God he served so totally. Fathers Peter and Diego, becoming uneasy as the minutes ticked on, glanced at each other. Ignatius seemed totally unaware of time or of his surroundings. As

"I will help you in Rome."

they watched him, his face suddenly became radiant. All the weariness, all the worry lines were gone. His eyes were wide and alert, and he leaned slightly forward as though he were receiving some message. His two companions watched in wonder, not daring to interrupt. Finally Ignatius seemed to relax back into his natural position.

Father Diego took advantage of the moment. Leaning over, he whispered, "Father, we must leave if we are to reach Rome before sunset."

Ignatius nodded but didn't raise his head. Quietly he rose and the three priests left the chapel. They were silent as they continued the journey. A few more miles and they would be in Rome.

The two younger priests couldn't help wondering what had happened back at the chapel. All they could do was wait for Ignatius to tell them about it. They did notice, though, that he seemed more peaceful than before.

Finally Ignatius murmured something inaudible.

"Did you say something, Father?" Father Peter asked.

"I was just commenting on how good God is to us, my brothers. While we were in the chapel, something amazing happened to me. I don't know what it is God wants us to do...perhaps we will die on the cross or suffer torments. But one thing I'm certain of, whatever happens, Jesus will stand by us as our friend."

"Father, what happened?"

"What vision did God grant you?"

Ignatius looked at the eager faces before him.

"While I was in prayer, I saw God the Father. Jesus was beside him with his cross on his shoulder. The Father asked Jesus if he would take me as his servant, and Jesus took me, saying, 'I want you to serve us.' Then God seemed to imprint these words on my heart: 'I will help you in Rome.'"

THE COMPANY OF JESUS

Ignatius and his two companions arrived in Rome at the end of 1537. Months passed. The war with the Turks continued and peace was nowhere in sight.

Ignatius, Peter, and Diego still hoped for the day when they could all set sail for Jerusalem to make their pilgrimage. They wrote weekly letters from Rome to their brothers working in the other Italian cities.

Pope Paul III himself had requested that Father Peter Favre and Father Diego Laynez teach courses at the Sapienza College in Rome. Once every two weeks the Pope even invited the two priests to dinner, so that he could hold theological discussions with them. As for Ignatius, the Pope had given him permission to continue his work of giving the Spiritual Exercises and preaching by word and example.

Sometime after Easter of 1538, Ignatius wrote to his companions throughout Italy asking them all to come to Rome. There they went about the city preaching, teaching, and helping the poor and sick in whatever ways they could.

Although he had been ordained a priest with his companions on June 24, 1537, Ignatius had postponed celebrating his first Mass. He did this out of humility and his great desire to prepare himself properly for this wonderful event. Ignatius finally offered his first Mass on Christmas Day, 1538, at the Basilica of Saint Mary Major, where a relic of the crib of Jesus was kept.

From that Christmas Eve until the end of May, a terrible frost gripped Italy. Blizzards, hail, and torrential downpours ruined crops. Soon famine struck the country. In Rome, the poor and homeless were dying in the streets. Ignatius and his men did all they could to help.

"Father Ignatius," one of the younger priests cried one day, "we can't take in any more people. The house is already full...with over two hundred of them! Where can we get enough food?"

"God will provide," Ignatius replied calmly. "Give them our beds, our food, but never turn anyone away."

Pope Paul III was very impressed with Ignatius and his men. They were not only intelligent and learned, they were holy. At that time there were many confusing ideas and false religious teachings circulating. Priests, brothers, and sisters were not always living up to Gospel ideals. The Church needed persons who would live and teach as Jesus had. Pope Paul saw that this is just what Ignatius and his companions were doing. Soon their reputation for holiness and knowledge spread. They were often called upon to help people recognize the difference between truth and error.

Pope Paul continued to invite some of Ignatius's men to visit him. One evening in 1539, as they discussed the life of Christ, their desire to go to the Holy Land came up in the conversation.

"Why do you want to go to Jerusalem?" the Pope asked. "Can't you see that Rome is a true Jerusalem for you if you want to serve God and work for the Church?"

Those words were reported back to Ignatius. He prayed and thought about the will of God. He began to understand more clearly what God wanted of him and his followers. They would place themselves completely at the service of the Pope. They would do whatever he asked—for the greater glory of God.

Little by little, Ignatius and his companions realized that they needed to be better organized in order to do more good. They held many discussions. They finally came to the decision that it would be best for them to form a new religious order in the Church.

"What should we call ourselves?" one in the group asked.

Ignatius thought a moment. He traveled back in memory to the military company he had led so many years before.

"We're a company of soldiers," he said slowly, "fighting for the salvation of every man, woman and child. Our Captain is Jesus and under his banner we will march forward. I propose," he concluded, "that we call ourselves the Company of Jesus!"

"Yes! Yes!"

"A perfect name, Father!"

The vote was unanimous and the name was accepted.

After more prayer and discussion, the men wrote up a plan of life for themselves and submitted it to the Pope for his approval. This plan, called the Constitutions, specified that besides the usual vows of chastity, poverty and obedience made by all religious, they would also make a vow of obedience to the Pope. They would instruct people in the Catholic faith, paying special attention to the Christian education of children. They would preach and serve others in whatever ways the Pope thought best.

On September 27, 1540, the papal document authorizing the foundation of the new order was published, and the Company (also called the Society) of Jesus was officially born.

16

CHOOSING A GENERAL

One of the first tasks awaiting the Company of Jesus was to elect a leader from among the group. New recruits had joined, but only the original members were to take part in the election of their superior.

Just a handful of the first members were present in March of 1541 for the election, since several of the priests were already in mission lands. Father Francis Xavier and Father Rodriguez were in Portugal, but both had left their sealed ballots behind. Father Peter Favre was in Germany. He sent his vote by way of a messenger.

After three days of praying for God's guidance, each priest wrote the name of his choice on a slip of paper. Then all the ballots, including the ballots of those who were absent, were placed in a box. One by one they were then opened and read:

"Father Ignatius."

"Father Ignatius."

"Father Ignatius."

Every ballot, except Ignatius's, bore the same name!

Ignatius was alarmed. "I can't accept. My health is too weak; I'm an old man now. I'm not suitable to be the superior...my past is filled with sin."

"Father," his companions encouraged, "God has seen fit to begin our Company through you."

"There is no one more capable of guiding us than yourself."

"The Lord will help you!"

Still Ignatius protested. "You think too highly of me. I'm calling for a new election. Yes, there must be a new election!"

His followers, saddened to see Ignatius so disturbed, agreed to hold another election on April 13th.

The result was the same. Ignatius was unanimously named superior general of the new order.

"Will you accept, Father?"

"Please, choose another," Ignatius begged.

Father Diego stood up. "If you don't accept, I'm leaving the Company!" he declared. "I believe God has chosen you to be our superior!"

"Let me ask the advice of my confessor," Ignatius finally pleaded.

The men agreed. After several more days the confessor's decision came: Ignatius should accept the office of superior.

The Company of Jesus had its first general.

17

SETTING THE WORLD ON FIRE

On April 22, 1541, Ignatius and the five companions who were with him in Rome visited seven of the most famous churches of the city. At the Basilica of Saint Paul they all received the sacrament of Reconciliation. After that, Ignatius celebrated Mass for them. Just before Communion, Ignatius, with tears in his eyes and holding the sacred Host in his hand, made the vows of chastity, poverty and obedience for all his life. He also vowed special obedience to the Pope. One by one his companions pronounced these same vows in the Company of Jesus.

Pope Paul III was grateful to have these new missionaries to send to other lands. Soon the "Jesuits," as they were nicknamed, were branching out to Portugal, France, Germany, India and Ireland. Everywhere they went they worked wonders by giving the Spiritual Exercises and teaching and preaching about Jesus.

Soon more young men were asking to join the Company, and a more structured life was needed. In 1550 Ignatius founded the Roman College, known today as the Gregorian University. It welcomed and educated young lay men as well as new members of the order.

At the end of that year, Ignatius's health took a turn for the worse. He penned a letter to his spiritual sons and called them together on January 30, 1551.

"This letter," he explained slowly, "contains something about which I've been thinking for months, even years. I'm older now and too sickly to continue in the position of superior general. I ask you to release me from this office."

Cries of protest rose immediately.

"Father, we can't accept your resignation! Please don't ask us to do such a thing!"

Ignatius was visibly moved by the reaction. Without a word, he accepted the decision of his sons. They were right. He must not give up now. The next day he was back to work again.

In the following years the Company continued to grow and spread. The Jesuits were credited with astonishing conversions wherever they went. But it was Father Francis Xavier who became the most enthusiastic missionary of them all. In April of 1541

"Father, we can't accept your resignation!"

Ignatius had sent him to India. After a long sea journey he landed at Goa on May 6, 1542.

Francis had a wonderful voice and could memorize tunes easily. When he saw that he couldn't get the people to listen to his preaching, he came up with another idea. Francis took the tunes that the sailors sang and put new words to the notes. Now the songs were about Jesus and the teachings of his Church! He then proceeded to sing these songs up and down the coast. The sailors brought home the new words, their children picked them up, and soon Francis had many people asking to be taught about Jesus and his Gospel. Eventually, thousands asked Francis to baptize them.

After bringing the Gospel to the people of the inland areas, Francis moved on to Japan in 1549. He stayed there for two years. But his greatest desire was to penetrate the Great Wall of China...to pierce it for Christ. So once again he took to sea. In October of 1552, he landed on the island of Sancian, just six miles off the coast of mainland China. The weather was bitterly cold and Francis often had nothing to eat. At the end of November, he came down with a fever, which increased day by day. Francis died at Sancian—within sight of China—on December 3, 1552. He was forty-six years old.

No missionary has ever covered more territory, overcome more difficulties, or worked for God with more fervor and heroic sacrifice than Francis Xavier. The Church later canonized him, giving him the title "Apostle of the Indies."

The fire in Francis's heart had been captured by Ignatius, channeled and set free to enflame the world with the love of God. "Go, and set all things on fire," Ignatius had once told him. Until his death, Francis had made those words his personal mission.

18

"Let the Candle Burn Out"

Ignatius continued to work hard until the end of his life. He wrote over 6,000 letters, either personally or through his secretary, oversaw the founding of new colleges and universities in many countries, and had his Spiritual Exercises published in Rome with full papal approval. A Pope once observed that Ignatius helped form more saints with his Spiritual Exercises than the number of individual letters needed to print the book!

But as Ignatius grew older, the stomach pains he had always suffered on and off increased. Realizing that he might not live much longer, the members of his Company begged him to tell them the story of his life.

One priest, Father Nadal, was especially determined to get Ignatius to tell his story. "Father, it would benefit the whole congregation," he argued.

"No," came Ignatius's answer. But Father Nadal wasn't one to give up easily. He and two other companions continued to ask until Ignatius simply said, "Celebrate three Masses, and I will tell you my decision."

Each of the priests offered three Masses, then went back to Ignatius. Again the answer was, "No."

Father Nadal was exasperated: "Father! It's been four years now that I've been asking you to write your memoirs, not only in my name, but in the name of all the members of our Society. Please explain to us how God formed you from the first day of your conversion."

"No," Ignatius once again replied. Actually, he had secretly already begun to tell Father Gonzales de Camara his story, but he didn't want anyone to know it. Even so, Father Gonzales had a difficult time getting anything out of the superior general. He was forced to remind Ignatius every day about his promise to tell the story. Ignatius always seemed to have one excuse or another.

Finally, Ignatius summoned Gonzales and gave him an account of his life, up to the days of his stay at Manresa. Gonzales wrote everything down. Then there was silence for over a year. The priest could get nothing more from Ignatius, even though he kept begging him to finish the story. Ignatius eventually told him everything, and Fathers Nadal and Polanco published Father Gonzales' manuscript.

Ignatius's health continued to fail. The terrible pains in his stomach left him exhausted. Father Madrid (who was also a doctor) and Doctor Petronio visited him on July 29, 1556. Although Ignatius was in great pain and there was nothing they could do for him, they didn't think it was the end. "He will probably survive this crisis as he has the others," they commented.

But Ignatius knew otherwise. The next day, Thursday, he called Father Polanco.

"The end of my life is approaching. Go and ask the Pope's blessing and recommend the Society to his care. If I am admitted into heaven, by God's mercy, I promise my prayers for him."

Father Polanco was surprised to hear Ignatius speaking like this. "Father," he responded, "I wanted to finish some urgent letters for Spain this evening. May my trip to the Vatican wait until morning?"

"The sooner you go, the happier I will be," answered Ignatius. "But do as you think best."

This placed the priest in a quandary. It disturbed him to think that Ignatius felt he was going to die, when the doctors didn't seem to agree. Father Polanco went back to one of the physicians. Since he was again assured that Ignatius showed no alarming symptoms, he decided to postpone the Vatican trip until the following morning.

That evening Father Polanco and Father Madrid stayed with Ignatius as he had his supper. Ignatius seemed to be in good spirits and they carried on a lively conversation, even discussing a house they were thinking of buying for the Company.

That night, Brother Thomas Cannicaro, the infirmarian, remained with Ignatius. He noticed nothing unusual. "Leave the candle burning, Thomas. Let it go out by itself," Ignatius directed before drifting off to sleep.

A few times during the night Brother Thomas heard Ignatius sigh, "Oh, Jesus!" But it was the founder's custom to offer such short prayers, so the infirmarian thought nothing of it.

At daybreak, Thomas went to open the shuttered windows. In the dim light he was shocked to see that Ignatius appeared to be dying! Quickly he rang the bell. Some of the priests came running, while Father Polanco rushed to the Vatican to ask the Holy Father's blessing. But by the time he returned, the man who had spent his life for the greater glory of God had already gone peacefully home to him. It was Friday, July 31, 1566.

Father Polanco immediately sent out letters to all the Jesuits informing them of the death of their father and founder. One of them, Father Ribadeneira, wrote back: "He has been too wonderful an example here on earth not to be a great intercessor before the Lord in heaven. In our hearts we say, 'Saint Ignatius, pray for us!'"

Pope Gregory XV officially canonized Ignatius on May 22, 1622.

We celebrate his feast day each year on July 31.

Prayer

Saint Ignatius, you loved excitement, adventures and challenges. And you found them all when you handed your life over to God.

Once you wrote a prayer surrendering everything you had to God—your freedom, your memory, your understanding, and even your will. All you asked for in return was God's love and grace.

Help me to realize that when I have God and his love, I have everything. I want to listen to God in my heart as you did. I want to say yes to whatever he asks of me. Help me to live the Gospel and to follow Jesus as closely as you did. Pray for me, Saint Ignatius. Amen.

GLOSSARY

1. **Annunciation, Feast of the**—the day (usually March 25) on which the Church celebrates: 1) the Archangel Gabriel's announcement to Mary that God had chosen her to be the Mother of his Son; 2) Mary's agreement to become the Mother of God's Son, and 3) the moment in which God the Son, the Second Person of the Blessed Trinity, took a human body and soul in Mary's womb through the power of the Holy Spirit, becoming the God-man, Jesus Christ.

2. **Canonize**—the act by which the Pope declares that a deceased person has lived Christian virtues to an heroic degree, is now in heaven, and may be honored by the whole Church. **Canonization** is the name given to the ceremony in which a person is declared a saint.

3. **Chivalry**—a term used to describe the qualities of a knight, which included: courage, kindness, fairness, respect for women, and a concern for the protection of the poor.

4. **Company** (as the term is used in this book)—a group of soldiers.

5. **Confessor** (as the term is used in this book)—a priest to whom one confesses one's sins in the sacrament of Reconciliation.

6. **Don**—in Spain and other Spanish-speaking countries, a title of respect used before a man's name.

7. **Doña**—in Spain and other Spanish-speaking countries, a title of respect used before a married woman's name.

8. **Fasting**—going without food. By giving up food for a short time, a person offers God a sacrifice and shows that he or she depends only on him.

9. **Grace**—God's own life in our soul.

10. **Heresy**—a denial of a truth of the Catholic faith.

11. **Humility**—the virtue of modesty or meekness; the opposite of pride.

12. **Knight**—in medieval times, a man, usually of noble birth, who was given an honorary military title by the king or by another high-ranking lord.

13. **Monastery**—the place where monks or nuns live as a community, dedicating themselves to a life of prayer.

14. **Page**—in medieval times, a boy servant of a nobleman.

15. **Penance**—a prayer or action that a person says or does to express to God his or her sorrow for sin.

16. **Pilgrim**—a person who travels to a holy place to pray and to feel closer to God. The journey he or she makes is called a **pilgrimage**.

17. **Religious** (as a noun)—men or women who are consecrated to God by the vows (special promises) of chastity, poverty and obedience. These persons live together and carry out some form of service for the people of God.

18. **Sackcloth**—a very rough kind of cloth used to make sacks and also worn by persons in past times as a sign of sorrow for their sins or their desire to do penance.

19. **Vigil**—a time of keeping watch during the night. As it is used in this book, a *vigil* was a night spent in prayer.

Who are the Daughters of St. Paul?

We are Catholic sisters with a mission. Our task is to bring the love of Jesus to everyone like Saint Paul did. You can find us in over 50 countries. Our founder, Blessed James Alberione, showed us how to reach out to the world through the media. That's why we publish books, make movies and apps, record music, broadcast on radio, perform concerts, help people at our bookstores, visit parishes, host JClub book fairs, use social media and the Internet, and pray for all of you.

Visit our Web site at www.pauline.org

BOOKS & MEDIA

The Daughters of St. Paul operate book and media centers at the following addresses. Visit, call, or write the one nearest you today, or find us at www.paulinestore.org.

CALIFORNIA
3908 Sepulveda Blvd, Culver City, CA 90230   310-397-8676
3250 Middlefield Road, Menlo Park, CA 94025   650-562-7060

FLORIDA
145 S.W. 107th Avenue, Miami, FL 33174   305-559-6715

HAWAII
1143 Bishop Street, Honolulu, HI 96813   808-521-2731

ILLINOIS
172 North Michigan Avenue, Chicago, IL 60601   312-346-4228

LOUISIANA
4403 Veterans Memorial Blvd, Metairie, LA 70006   504-887-7631

MASSACHUSETTS
885 Providence Hwy, Dedham, MA 02026   781-326-5385

MISSOURI
9804 Watson Road, St. Louis, MO 63126   314-965-3512

NEW YORK
115 E. 29th Street, New York City, NY 10016   212-754-1110

SOUTH CAROLINA
243 King Street, Charleston, SC 29401   843-577-0175

VIRGINIA
1025 King Street, Alexandria, VA 22314   703-549-3806

CANADA
3022 Dufferin Street, Toronto, ON M6B 3T5   416-781-9131

¡También somos su fuente para libros,
videos y música en español!